Little Stars

A CRABTREE SEEDLINGS BOOK

Taylor Farley

I am in ski school!

I wear warm clothes.

scarf
jacket
gloves
ski pants

I wear a helmet, goggles, ski boots, and **skis**.

helmet
goggles
ski boot
skis

bindings

My ski boots clip into the **bindings**.

Some of us use **ski poles**.

ski poles

We **practice** the right way to fall.

We practice how to get up again!

We learn to form a **wedge**.

We learn to turn
and stop.

Time to go down the **bunny hill**!

BURTON
BURTON

Glossary

bindings (BYN-dings): Bindings are attached to the skis and grip the boots.

bunny hill (BUH-nee HIL): A bunny hill is an easy hill where children and beginning skiers learn to ski.

practice (PRAK-tiss): Practice is doing something over and over for improvement.

ski poles (SKEE POLES): Skiers use ski poles for balance and for extra push.

skis (SKEEZ): Skis are long, narrow pieces of hard material. People wear skis to glide over snow.

wedge (WEDJ): A wedge is formed when the front tips of the skis point together and the ends of the skis are wide apart.

Index

School-to-Home Support for Caregivers and Teachers

Crabtree Seedlings books help children grow by letting them practice reading. Here are a few guiding questions to help the reader build his or her comprehension skills. Possible answers are included.

Before Reading

- **What do I think this book is about?** I think this book is about skiing. It might tell us about how children learn to ski.
- **What do I want to learn about this topic?** I want to learn about the clothing a person wears when skiing.

During Reading

- **I wonder why...** I wonder why some skiers use ski poles and some do not.
- **What have I learned so far?** I learned that skiers wear warm clothes, such as scarves, jackets, gloves, and ski pants. They also wear a helmet, goggles, ski boots, and skis.

After Reading

- **What details did I learn about this topic?** I learned that skiers go to ski school to learn the right way to fall, how to make a wedge, and how to turn and stop.
- **Write down unfamiliar words and ask questions to help understand their meaning.** I see the word *bindings* on page 9 and the word *practice* on page 12. The other vocabulary words are listed on pages 22 and 23.

Library and Archives Canada Cataloguing in Publication

Title: Little stars skiing / Taylor Farley.
Other titles: Skiing
Names: Farley, Taylor, author.
Description: Series statement: Little stars | "A Crabtree seedlings book". | Includes index. |
Previously published in electronic format by Blue Door Education in 2020.
Identifiers: Canadiana 20200379771 | ISBN 9781427129857 (hardcover) | ISBN 9781427130037 (softcover)
Subjects: LCSH: Skis and skiing—Juvenile literature.
Classification: LCC GV854.315 .F37 2021 | DDC j796.93—dc23

Library of Congress Cataloging-in-Publication Data

Names: Farley, Taylor, author.
Title: Little stars skiing / Taylor Farley.
Other titles: Skiing
Description: New York, NY : Crabtree Publishing Company, [2021] | Series: Little stars: a Crabtree seedlings book | Includes index.
Identifiers: LCCN 2020049358 | ISBN 9781427129857 (hardcover) | ISBN 9781427130037 (paperback)
Subjects: LCSH: Skis and skiing--Juvenile literature.
Classification: LCC GV854.315 .F37 2021 | DDC 796.93--dc23
LC record available at https://lccn.loc.gov/2020049358

e-book ISBN 978-1-949354-08-9

Print book version produced jointly with Blue Door Education in 2021

Printed in the Canada/052022/CPC20220512

Photo credits: Cover and pages 5, 7, 11, 18 © FamVeld; Pages 2-3 © NataliaVo; page 8 © Tomsickova Tatyana; page 13 © Julia Kuznetsova; page 14 © Petr Bonek; page 17 © Kaca Skokanova; pages 20-21 © YanLev
All photos from Shutterstock.com